Contents

Written by Kyle Taylor and Lisa Rajan

Illustrated by Sawyer Cloud

Collins

1 The internet

Sam and Layla are best friends. They go to the same school, they live on the same street and they even share the same birthday!

For as long as they can remember, Sam and Layla have enjoyed spending time together.

They like using their imaginations to go on fun adventures. They've been astronauts rocketing to the moon.

They've been deep-sea explorers diving down to the ocean floor.

This time, they are going on a whole new kind of adventure. Sam and Layla are going online to use the **internet**.

They know that they use "**wi-fi**" to connect to each other "over the internet". But what is wi-fi? And what is the internet?

Wi-fi is a way for phones, **tablets**, computers and other devices to connect to the internet without needing cables.

Did you know?

The internet is mostly made up of 885,000 kilometres of underground and underwater cables. The internet is like roads that connect towns and cities.

If you laid all the cables that make up the internet end to end, they would go around Earth 14 times!

Giant cables like these lie on the ground of the ocean and carry digital information across Earth to make the internet work.

Sam and Layla like watching TV programmes and videos. They like playing console games with each other too, especially Karting Krayze Racing. That got Sam and Layla wondering ... could they do these things on the internet as well?

Did you know?

The **World Wide Web**, or "www", is all the **webpages** you find on the internet, like houses on the roads connecting the towns.

The information on the webpages is called **data** – letters, numbers and pictures. It's like the people in the cars on the roads.

Every webpage has its own unique address, much like houses do, so that anyone can find it from any computer in the world.

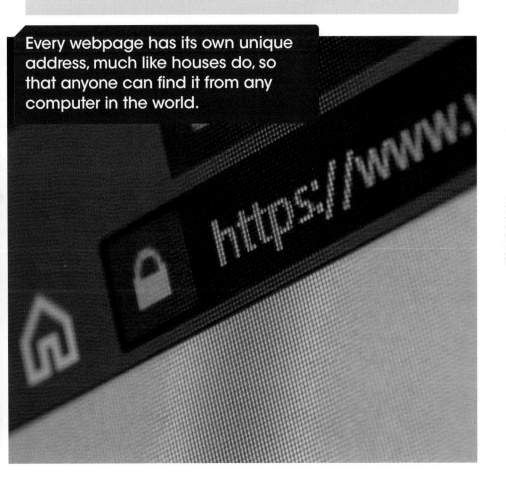

2 Coding

Sam and Layla want to know how people tell computers what to do. What language do computers speak?

> The languages people speak have lots of different words in them. Computers speak **machine language**, which only has two "words": "0" and "1".
>
> "0" means "no data" and "1" means "yes data".

Combinations of 1s and 0s instruct a computer to do different things: from making a letter appear on screen when you press it on the keyboard ... to programming a game or making a **website**.

These instructions are called **binary code**. People who program computers are called **coders**.

```
252        document.getElementById(bigImageDesc).inner
253    }
254
255    function updatePhotoDescription() {
256        if (descriptions.length > (page * 9) + (current
257            document.getElementById(bigImageDesc)
258        }
259    }
260
261    function updateAllImages() {
262        var i = 1;
263        while (i < 10) {
264            var elementId = 'foto' + i;
265            var elementIdBig = 'bigImage' + i;
266            if (page * 9 + i - 1 < photos.length) {
267                document.getElementById( elem
268                document.getElementById( elem
           } else {
               document.getElementById( el
           }
       }
```

A coder writes in machine language.

Sam and Layla learnt that to make a letter from the alphabet, you put eight 0s and 1s together. Different combinations of 0s and 1s make different letters.

"What would our names be in machine language?" Sam asked Layla.

Sam and Layla realised that even though their names are different, they look similar in machine language!

Try it!

Now you know how it works, can you use the chart below to spell your name in machine language and write like a computer?

Character	Binary code	Character	Binary code
A	01000001	N	01001110
B	01000010	O	01001111
C	01000011	P	01010000
D	01000100	Q	01010001
E	01000101	R	01010010
F	01000110	S	01010011
G	01000111	T	01010100
H	01001000	U	01010101
I	01001001	V	01010110
J	01001010	W	01010111
K	01001011	X	01011000
L	01001100	Y	01011001
M	01001101	Z	01011010

This translation chart shows you what the binary code is for each capital letter.

3 The online you

"Shall we play a game together online?"
Layla suggested to Sam.

"My brother plays a really fun game where you make
your own zoo," said Sam.

"Yes! My sister plays it too. You team up with other
players to find jewels and coins to buy the funny
creatures to put in your zoo," said Layla excitedly.

Sam and Layla touched the app to start the game.
The first thing to do was design their player characters
– virtual versions of themselves called **avatars**.
Layla made her character look as much like her
as possible.

Sam designed his character. "I'm going to have some fun with this," he said.

When they had both finished, Sam and Layla showed each other their avatars.

Username: battledragon456
Age: 456
From: THE MOON

"That doesn't look like you, and you're not from the moon," said Layla. "You're lying."

"But I don't want anyone on the internet to know where I am or what I really look like," replied Sam. "If I use a nickname, and say I'm from a funny place, it's much safer."

What do you think?

Should your avatar look like you?

Was Sam being safe or should he have been more truthful?

Are other people always who they say they are online?

Can you always trust what you see online?

4 Be aware

PING!

Layla got a **notification** on her tablet. How exciting! Someone wanted to add her as a "friend" on the game, but she didn't know who it was.

Sam leant over and tried to tap "Yes", but Layla moved her screen away.

"I don't know who that person is," Layla told Sam.

"It's just someone to play the game with online," Sam shrugged. "And you might know her?"

"How do we know this person is a girl?" said Layla. "We don't know who this really is. I don't know her real name, so how can I tell?"

choosing a username and designing an avatar

Before Layla could decide what to do, a message appeared from Cutepuppy33.

Hi, it's Robin. I love this game. I have lots of the zoo animals as real toys too. We could play with them together. Where do you live?

Sam and Layla looked at each other.

"All your friends know where you live, Layla," said Sam. "That person doesn't know you."

"So why are they making friends with me?" asked Layla. They both felt a bit uncomfortable about it.

What should they do?

1. Don't reply.
2. Don't ignore the message.
3. Tell and show an adult they trust.

Anybody can pretend to be someone else online.

Did you know?

Being wary of people you don't know online is just as important as it is offline.

People don't have to tell the truth about themselves online.

They told Layla's mum. She knew straight away that "Robin" wasn't a friend.

"You were right to come and tell me," she said. "You should always tell an adult you trust when something happens online that you are not sure about."

"Even if you think it's OK," continued Layla's mum, "the safest thing to do is talk about it with an adult you trust, like a parent, grandparent or teacher."

Staying safe on the internet ...

Remember, friends that you only know online are still strangers.

It's best to only use the internet when a trusted adult is around.

Always tell an adult if you are not sure about something.

Tell a trusted adult if you receive a message from someone that makes you feel uncomfortable.

5 You choose

Layla's mum helped her block the player who left the message. They decided to leave the game for now and watch videos instead.

"What do you want to search for?" asked Layla's mum.

"I know!" said Layla, typing into the search box.

They clicked on one of the results. A video started playing.

"Is this the video we chose?" Layla asked Sam, confused.

"No ... I think it's an **advert**," said Sam. "It does have a cat in it though."

Did you know?

Companies that sell things pay websites to show their advert before you watch the videos you want.

HOME

AMAZING DEALS!!!
>>CLICK HERE<<

Adverts online can be boxes of text that pop up, or videos that play automatically. Many include a button or text to click on to take you to another website.

Once the advert video finished, the cat video they wanted began to play. It was very funny.

When it ended, another video began playing. It was also quite funny. Then a third video. By the fourth, the videos were not funny anymore. In fact, they were making Sam and Layla feel uncomfortable.

Did you know?

Many websites have an **autoplay** feature that automatically starts another video.

This is to keep you watching videos for as long as possible.

That way, they can show you more adverts.

The more videos you watch, the less they will be like the one you searched for.

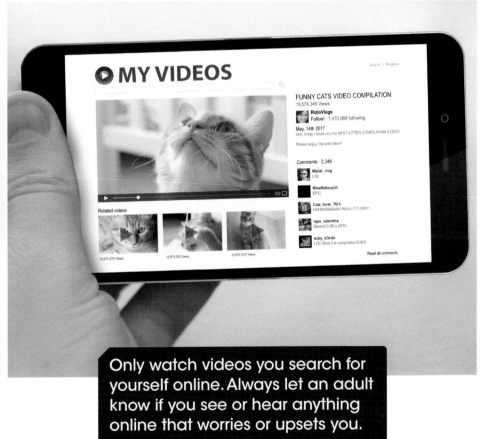

Only watch videos you search for yourself online. Always let an adult know if you see or hear anything online that worries or upsets you.

6 Screen time

"Screen time is up," said Layla's mum.
Sam and Layla looked at each other, surprised.
"It can't be!" Sam said.

"You've been online together for two hours," Layla's mum told him. "What have you been doing?"

"I watched videos," smiled Layla.

"I played games," beamed Sam.

What do you think?

Were Sam and Layla really spending time together?

Is two hours a long time to spend online?

Is playing games better than watching videos?

Should they spend all their screen time doing just one activity?

What else could you spend your screen time doing?

"Please can we have some more screen time, Mum?" asked Layla.

"I wanted to watch some videos and I didn't get a chance to," complained Sam.

"Our screen time goes by so fast," said Layla. "It's not long enough!"

It's easy to lose track of time when you're online.

"Why don't you plan how you spend your screen time tomorrow?" suggested Layla's mum. "Then you'll be able to do everything you want to in the time you have."

learn about planets

watch funny
dog videos

play Karting
Krayze Racing

message Patrick
and Grace

find ideas for my
birthday list

7 True or false?

The following day, Sam and Layla spent all morning playing in the garden. Then they decided to have some screen time. They looked at their lists to remind themselves of what they wanted to do online. They shared one screen so they could do things together.

Sam and Layla decided to start with learning about the planets. They searched for "solar system" on the internet and clicked on one of the links that came up.

It was a website about planets, but something didn't seem right. The planets on this website looked different to the ones in Layla's book about the solar system.

Why was that?

Planets in our solar system. Or are they?

"Do you think it's true?" Layla asked Sam.

"I don't know," said Sam. "It looks real, but there are some clues that make me think it's fake."

How to spot something unreliable ...

Spelling mistakes?

Sentences that don't make sense?

Words like "promoted", "advert" or "sponsored"?

Links to buying things?

Forms asking for your personal information?

Not finding the same information on other websites?

Science

The internet is a great way to learn new things but not everything online is true, so always check in other places to make sure.

8 Bullying online

Next on Sam and Layla's list was messaging their friends. Sam replied to a message from his friend Patrick at school. Patrick asked Sam what he was doing.

Patrick started messaging Layla. She was surprised, because Patrick never talked to her at school.
His messages weren't very nice. He said that she was rubbish at football and that nobody at school liked playing with her. This made Layla feel sad and hurt.

Did you know?

Bullying someone online is called **cyberbullying** or online bullying.

It can be just as hurtful as bullying in real life.

Mean messages can be upsetting.

Sam felt angry at Patrick for being mean to Layla.

"I'm going to message him back and say something nasty to him. That will get him back for being horrible to you," Sam told Layla.

"No, don't," she replied. "Then you will be a bully too."

"Is it bullying, though?" Sam asked. "It's only words. I'm not actually hurting him."

What is cyberbullying or online bullying?

Sending mean messages to or about someone.

Keep on messaging when you've been asked to stop.

Writing things about someone that aren't true.

Pretending to be someone else.

Taking or sharing embarrassing photos.

There are lots of different kinds of online bullying.

Sam and Layla told Layla's mum about Patrick.

"I'm glad you didn't write something mean back to Patrick," said Layla's mum. "You would be in trouble for cyberbullying too."

"Not if I delete the message afterwards," said Sam.

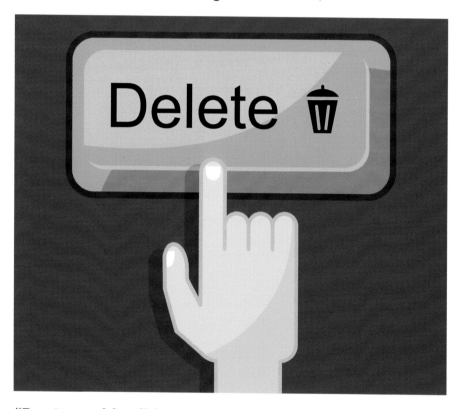

"But it would still be on Patrick's tablet," Layla's mum pointed out. "And your behaviour online is just as important as your behaviour offline. You must think carefully about everything you do, as it's still linked to you."

Online behaviour includes ...

Videos you watch

Pictures you look at

Comments you leave

Websites you visit

Messages you send

Links you click on

Things you buy online

Your online activity leaves a trace.

9 Staying safe and happy

"I'm glad you talked to me when something happened online that made you feel worried or uncomfortable," smiled Layla's mum. "You should always tell an adult you trust – a parent, grandparent, teacher or family friend."

"It made us feel much better," said Sam, "because adults know what to do."

"I don't like it when things happen that I don't understand," added Layla. "It spoils my fun!"

"Whatever happens online, I'll never be cross with you," said Layla's mum. "And I'll always help."

Always ...

If something makes you feel sad, worried or angry, tell and show an adult you trust.

"Do you think people behave differently when they are online?" asked Layla's mum.

Layla and Sam thought about it.

"I don't think Patrick would say mean things to me in real life," said Layla.

"I don't think I'd get angry about losing a race in real life," said Sam.

Remember ...

Online activities can affect your mood or feelings.

You might react differently to how you were expecting.

Layla's tablet was running out of charge. She plugged it in.

"I love going online and I thought it would always make me happy," Layla said to Sam. "I didn't realise some things would make me worry."

"Same here," agreed Sam. "But now that we know what to do if something unexpected happens, I feel much safer doing all the things I enjoy."

Glossary

advert a picture or video encouraging you to buy something

autoplay another video starts playing automatically at the end of the first one

avatars characters representing people in a video game

binary code a language using 0s and 1s to represent letters and numbers

coders people who write code for computer programs

cyberbullying bullying someone using online messages

data the bits of information stored by a computer

internet a global network connecting computers, smartphones, tablets and other devices together

machine language the way computers communicate with each other

notification an alert that you have a message

tablets small mobile computers with a large touch screen

webpage a page of information on a website

website a group of pages online that let you buy something, find something out or play a game

wi-fi allows computers, smartphones, tablets or other devices to connect to the internet without cables

World Wide Web the information, pictures and videos on the internet

Index

How did the online activities make us feel?

Messaging friends makes me feel popular and liked.

I was upset when a friend said mean things about me.

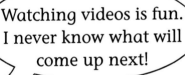

Watching videos is fun. I never know what will come up next!

Some of the videos made me feel confused and worried.

Ideas for reading

Written by Christine Whitney

Primary Literacy Consultant

Reading objectives:

- be introduced to non-fiction books that are structured in different ways
- listen to, discuss and express views about non-fiction
- retrieve and record information from non-fiction
- discuss and clarify the meanings of words

Spoken language objectives:

- participate in discussion
- speculate, hypothesise, imagine and explore ideas through talk
- ask relevant questions

Curriculum links: Computing: Use technology safely and respectfully; Writing: Write for different purposes

Word count: 2603

Interest words: cyberspace, internet, coding, avatar, autoplay, cyberbullying

Resources: paper, pencils and crayons, access to the internet

Build a context for reading

- Ask the group to share how much *screen time* they are allowed each day at home. Have they ever played any online games? If so, which ones?
- Show the title of the book. Ask for a volunteer to explain the meaning of the word *cyberspace*.
- Together, read the blurb on the back cover of the book. Ask children why it might be that Sam and Layla *don't always enjoy screen time as much as they think they will*.

Understand and apply reading strategies

- Read Chapter 1 together and ask children to explain what the *internet* is.
- Continue to read to the end of Chapter 3. Ask the group to discuss the question on page 15, *Can you always trust what you see online?*
- Read on to the end of Chapter 4. Ask children to explain why Sam and Layla *felt a bit uncomfortable* about the notification Layla received.